ISBN 978-1-333-08071-6
PIBN 10042236

1 MONTH OF
FREE
READING

at

www.ForgottenBooks.com

By purchasing this book you are
eligible for one month membership to
ForgottenBooks.com, giving you
unlimited access to our entire
collection of over 1,000,000 titles via
our web site and mobile apps.

To claim your free month visit:

www.forgottenbooks.com/free42236

English
Français
Deutsche
Italiano
Español
Português

www.forgottenbooks.com

Mythology Photography **Fiction**
Fishing Christianity **Art** Cooking
Essays Buddhism Freemasonry
Medicine **Biology** Music **Ancient**
Egypt Evolution Carpentry Physics
Dance Geology **Mathematics** Fitness
Shakespeare **Folklore** Yoga Marketing
Confidence Immortality Biographies
Poetry **Psychology** Witchcraft
Electronics Chemistry History **Law**
Accounting **Philosophy** Anthropology
Alchemy Drama Quantum Mechanics
Atheism Sexual Health **Ancient History**
Entrepreneurship Languages Sport
Paleontology Needlework Islam
Metaphysics Investment Archaeology
Parenting Statistics Criminology
Motivational

THE

FUTURE OF EDUCATED WOMEN,

By HELEN EKIN STARRETT;

AND

MEN, WOMEN, AND MONEY,

By FRANCES EKIN ALLISON.

CHICAGO:

JANSEN, McCLURG, AND COMPANY.

1885.

TO THE MEMORY OF

OUR FATHER,

THE LATE REV. JOHN EKIN, D.D.,

WHO, MORE THAN A QUARTER OF A CENTURY AGO, LOOKING
UPON HIS FAMILY OF FIVE DAUGHTERS, THOUGHT
OUT, FAR IN ADVANCE OF HIS CONTEMPO-
RARIES, ALL THE CONCLUSIONS EM-
BODIED IN THESE ESSAYS,

THEY ARE AFFECTIONATELY DEDICATED BY

HIS DAUGHTERS.

THE
FUTURE OF EDUCATED WOMEN.

During the year 1878 there appeared in that highly esteemed English periodical, *The Nineteenth Century*, two notable articles written by two representative English women, Mrs. Sutherland Orr, and Mrs. Milicent Garrett Fawcett, wife of the eminent Prof. Fawcett, which were, apparently, a summing up of all that is to be said pro and con on that subject which, as Mrs. Fawcett says, for want of a better name, is called "The Woman Question." The article by Mrs. Sutherland Orr entitled "The Future of English Women" was republished by the Appletons in the final issue of their supplement to the *Popular Science Monthly*. Mrs. Fawcett's article in reply to Mrs. Orr has never, I believe, been republished in this country, but both articles attracted very wide attention at the time and excited much comment both among English and American readers. Ever since their appearance I have expected that some student of sociology and observer of the evolution of society

would take up and point out more fully the fundamental weakness of the first article on the Future
of English Women, and also add somewhat to the
reply of Mrs. Fawcett.   No such attempt, in so
far as I know, has yet been made; and believing
that in reality the vitalest reason of "the movement" has not yet been fully set forth nor its most
important consequences foreseen or predicted, I
bring my contribution of observation, experience
and conviction towards the farther solution of the
problem.   That it is one of the most important
problems engaging the attention of thoughtful men
and women cannot be doubted, involving as it does
the right adjustment of the complex relations of
women to social and domestic life and the compen-
satory employments of civilized society.

The article on the Future of English Women by
Mrs. Sutherland Orr purports to be a calm, dispas-
sionate, philosophical consideration of the certain
results of what she is pleased to call "female emancipation;" this being accomplished as she avers by
the full admission of women to the medical pro
fession.   She says, and truly:

"When once the medical profession has been
thrown open to women the question of sexual dis-
abilities is at an end.   The line which may still be
drawn between the female doctor whose functions

are exercised in the sick room and the woman whose professional arena would be the church, the law-court or the chamber of legislation, holds good in theory but will be found to be non-existent in practice. The suffrage may be withheld and if so there will be no female members in Parliament, and, what is more to the immediate point, no direct female influence in political life. But whether politically represented or not, the destiny of women will be the same. They will triumph by reason of their social independence, which will be an indirect political power. Directly or indirectly, actually or potentially, for good or for evil, the battle for female emancipation will have been won."

The whole drift of Mrs. Orr's long and carefully considered article is to prove that it will be for evil. She very candidly admits that up to a certain point the movement for the emancipation of women has been a beneficent one; she admits that thus far it has borne excellent fruit in the elevation of the character and intelligence of women; in enlarging the scope of their vision; in increasing their self-respect; and as a consequence commanding for them the increasing respect of men. Nevertheless she deplores that the leaders cannot be induced to call a halt; she laments that they do not see that they have gone far enough; she wishes they could be induced to stay the rising tide of progress and say, 'thus far and no farther;' for in her opinion, car-

ried to its logical conclusion, it will result in the
utter decomposition of society.   "Admitting," she
says, "that women will achieve all that it is prophe-
sied they will be able to achieve when all the occupations of life, all avenues to profitable employment,
all the learned professions are as free to them as to
men, and are carried on indifferently by men or
women, the ultimate result will be, they will not be
superior women, they will only be inferior men;"
and she adds: "The one fatal result of female
emancipation is this: that in its full and final
attainment not only the power of love in women,
but for either sex its possibility will have passed
away."

So extravagant a statement, and one so utterly
unsupported by proofs might well be passed by
with a mere smile but for the fact that it finds opportunity for utterance in a publication of such
high authority as *The Nineteenth Century*, and
also calls forth a careful reply from Mrs. Fawcett,
a lady equally eminent with her husband as a student of social and political economy. Mrs. Fawcett
very properly refutes this statement by a cita-
tion of facts.   Resorting, as all students of social science should, to the scientific method of
proof or disproof, she cites the case of the large
class of women in England from which female

servants are drawn. She says that practically these women are in this condition of emancipation so dreaded by Mrs. Orr. They work independently for a livelihood from their early youth; they are at an early age their own mistresses; they earn and control their own money; there is no pressure of any kind, either social or otherwise, put upon them to marry; they do, in many cases, hard muscular work, and yet they love and are loved, desire mates and are sought in marriage, marry and bear children just as do the women of even the most favored and protected classes, and she does not perceive that their natural instincts and affections are a whit less susceptible, or that they are any less faithful and tender in all the domestic relations of life on account of their independent and self-supporting lives.

But though this illustration may satisfactorily disprove this sweeping statement of Mrs. Orr's, we are yet obliged to admit that many of the most candid and just thinkers upon this subject, both men and women, among those who have the very best interests of humanity deeply at heart, feel many misgivings as to the ultimate result of the general entrance of women into all departments of the activities of life. Many yield the assent of reason but withhold the assent of feeling.

Their heads are convinced but their hearts shrink
from accepting the life of a worker as the best life
for woman. They perceive the necessities that
compel women to go out into the world to do battle
for themselves and earn their living; they depre-
cate the injustice that would add a single feather
to the weight which they may carry or the disad-
vantages they may labor under on account of their
sex; with the true chivalry of the nineteenth century they say, "Make the crooked places straight
and the rough places plain for these tender feet
which must perforce walk alone over the difficult
paths of life;" but they inwardly feel, "Oh, that
such necessity might not be laid upon them." They
regard the necessity simply as the result of an
abnormal condition of society, and the money-
making efforts of women only as an acceptance of
the lesser evil. In their hearts they would probably coincide with Mrs. Orr in her statement that
"We can think away the woman question simply
by imagining the proportion of our marrying men
to be as great as it once was." That is, if there
were but a good husband for every woman there
would be no such thing as "The Woman Movement."

And the advocates of the emancipation of women and of such a training and education for them

as shall fit them for all the activities of life, for self-support and for independence of men, in so far as supporting themselves is concerned, and of giving into their hands that power which helps to mould and compel society through possession of a voice in making its laws, occupy an inherently weak position if they argue for all these things *only* on the ground that they are necessary in order to protect women from the emergencies, the catastrophies, the abnormal conditions of life. Their opponents might very justly reply, "It is our duty, not to adapt and prepare women for abnormal conditions, but rather to work for such a re-organization of society as shall cause the abnormal conditions to disappear. The normal condition of woman is that of wife and mother; and the urging of women to independent careers and their education for and entrance upon money-making professions tends directly to the extension and perpetuation of an abnormal condition of society, and is therefore in direct opposition to the laws of nature, and to the highest and best social life."

But let us go a little farther back and see if it is not really a natural law, and not an external necessity that is at the bottom of this movement; and if so let us not conclude that nature is no longer to be trusted. Let us see if there are not immutable laws at work in the evolution of organized society, just as we have learned there are in the evolution of organized life, which shall enable us rightly to interpret this "woman movement" and solve our perplexities as to its ultimate beneficent results. The environment of woman has changed entirely with the progress of civilization. The law of organic life is that the individual and the species constantly adapt themselves to their environment. May it not be that this law of adaptation is so mightily at work in a plastic social condition that the changes effected by it are constantly apparent to the most casual observer? If there is a natural law of adaptation at work attempting to harmonize woman's nature with progressing and changing intellectual and social conditions let us learn if possible what it is. Let us see if a study of the nature of woman and of the conditions necessary to her well-being and happiness as an intellectually and morally developed being will not furnish us with a clue to the harmonizing of the apparently conflicting demands of life upon her.

First then we note that modern civilization has educated woman. All her natural and mental faculties have been permitted to expand, and have been cultivated and stimulated to active growth. Now, the first and the necessary immediate effect of the development of the natural faculties is a desire to use them. This is an immutable law of all life. Teach a child to read and a thirst for reading is developed; teach it to draw and it will seek gratification in representing objects on paper or canvas; teach it music and it will wish to sing or play upon an instrument; develop a love of knowledge and you have set in play forces and desires which nothing but death can still. Cultivate any or all of the natural faculties and at the same time is developed a wish for power and opportunity to use or express those faculties. It was the remark of a noble woman who had observed much of life and pondered long on the defective conditions and suppressive limitations of womanhood, and who was a most earnest student of the causes of the agitated and unrestful spirit of the social and domestic life of to-day, that "what woman needs is *opportunity for expression.*" No sage could more perfectly formulate the natural and rational demands of her being; nor can speech, it may be added, embody more correctly and epigrammatically the true spirit of the woman movement.

What woman needs is opportunity for expression. This we recognize both as a great philosophical and great practical truth. It is the truth concerning the nature not only of women, but of every intelligent, aspiring human being, man or woman. It contains a statement of the true conditions for the healthful development of human character for usefulness and happiness. It is indeed the essential problem of life and happiness formulated for direct and certain solution.

In the expression or exercise of our natural faculties we find content and happiness; in their repression we realize pain and deformity. The spiritual nature is informed with a growing, living force just as the physical nature is, and must have room for growth and exercise under penalties corresponding to those which result when the body is fettered in growth and restrained in action. Our natural faculties seek to express themselves *objectively* in *creative* work. Has any one an artistic faculty? Delight and repose of spirit are found in the exercise of that faculty in the expression of itself in music, in painting, in sculpture, in literature. Has any one a faculty for understanding the natural sciences? Repose and delight of spirit are found in the study and application of the principles of science. Has any one a faculty for organizing, for planning, for directing others, for acquiring property? Repose and content and delight of spirit are found in the exercise of such faculties. From their repression the result will be pain and unrest and deformity of spirit.

From our observation and study of these facts of our spiritual and intellectual natures we easily arrive at this generalization: As intelligent human beings we are happy in the exercise of our natural faculties through that mode of expression which is correlated by a result *outside of ourselves;* which results in *something;* which externalizes and embodies inward consciousness and spiritual activity; which results in achievement, in equilibration, in reaction, in embodied life.   Matthew Arnold says in his preface to Essays In Criticism, that "it is undeniable that the exercise of a creative power, that a free creative activity is the true function of man; it is proved to be so by man's finding in it his true happiness."   In this saying he has formulated the true theory of life for all intelligent human beings.   We are happy when we are working at that which produces *something;* which rewards us with tangible results.   One of the first things we observe in the natural development of the faculties of children is that they are happy when they are working towards the accomplishment of a particular object.   Whether it is in the making of a wagon with spools, or a doll, or a sled, or even demolishing some toy to see how it is made, we find that we have secured a child's content and happiness so long as a definite object inspires its labors.   This is

a law of intellectual life and growth, and it is inherent in both boys and girls, in both men and women. We are impelled to the exercise of our faculties, and we want to exercise them in such a way
as shall *embody* our ideas, shall accomplish a spe-
cific result. When our labor accomplishes this spe-
cific result there is a sense of reward that is a re-
storer from fatigue, a real spiritual and mental as
well as physical nutriment and tonic.

And it is in the endeavor to conform to this
law of nature in the midst of changing social
conditions, that we find the real, vital principle of
the "woman movement." The education of the faculties of woman prompts with all the force of the
immutability of natural law to new forms of expression. There is that within woman by virtue of
the fact that she is a human being that constantly
impels her to action—to work. The nature and direction of the activities in which she should engage
are clearly defined by nature. The parent who
has seen two beautiful infants of originally the same
size and bodily contour develop healthily under
the same regime, the one into a great muscular,
strong-limbed, sturdy, rough-skinned boy, the other
into a graceful, slender girl with round, small-boned
limbs, small hands and feet, and a skin of flower-
like delicacy and bloom, quickly and rightly con-

cludes that activities requiring great muscular strength, and exposure to wind and weather are not for the girl, and are for the boy.* But the wisely observant parent will not conclude that the activities of the girl child are to be restrained in any directions not indicated by nature. The girl will run and play and use her fingers and sing and draw, and her mental faculties will develop exactly as the boy's faculties develop. There will be no danger of two and two making five in the girl's arithmetic; her constructive faculties will be the same, just as her digestion is the same as her brother's, and the wise parent will not attempt to create any artificial distinctions. As they grow up together the same law will be observed to control both, namely, they will be happy and contented in proportion as they find satisfactory expression for their faculties.

Living in the present advanced age of the world they will probably be educated in the same universities—certainly in the same studies. They will assimilate the same truths. In the article by Mrs. Sutherland Orr she says that "one of the deplorable tendencies of the times is that towards educating boys and girls in the same schools to

* There are few parents in these days who will argue that the boy's superior physical strength gives him any inherent right to control or compel his sister, or that on account of the differences in their physical development her interests should be subserved to his.

think and feel alike." I should like to ask her what method she would suggest by which to teach them to think and feel differently. The object of thought is the perception of truth; the moral nature is cultivated that feeling may be just, humane, truthful. Perhaps we might teach girls to think differently from boys by having a different set of text books for them. We might teach the girls that the earth was square, and teach the boys that it was round. We might teach, say, the greenback theory to girls, and the hard money theory to boys; we might have the girls taught protectionist theories, and the boys free trade; we might teach the girls pity for all suffering creatures, and the boys vivisection; we might teach girls that truth and honesty are the principal things, and teach the boys that business is business, and that it is impossible to tell the truth in transacting it. In no other way that I can imagine can boys and girls be taught to think and feel differently on subjects where truth and morality—the principal things in life—are concerned. But to return. Their curriculum of school studies having been completed they stand side by side on commencement day with their diplomas in their hands, and it is a very different question that is presented to the girl from that presented to the boy when it is asked "What next?"

The question is easily answered for the boy.   In obedience to the law of his being he enters at once upon a life of happy rewarding activity.   His education has but furnished him with the tools wherewith to carve the fortune of life.   From henceforth he is to know the delight of using those cultivated faculties in *achieving*.   He may do whatever he finds delight in, and if he does it well, aside from the pecuniary reward he secures he will also have the approbation of the world.   But the girl—her faculties, too, are all alive and eager for expression—action.   Shall her parents say to her: My daughter your normal condition and destiny is that of wife and mother.   Come now and occupy yourself contentedly with domestic tasks until the happy youth appears who shall complete your destiny.

Can two laws of nature conflict?   By the law of the necessity for the expression of her faculties the girl will find that the penalty of their neglect or disuse is pain and discontent.   She will also find that to employ them without any special object in view is impossible. All the so-called feminine work of modern society (considered feminine because it commands no pay—results in nothing permanent or valuable) is vanity and vexation of spirit to the active minded, rightly educated girl. She imagines how her educated brother would feel fooling away his time in the occupations allotted by society to her. Is it replied that this is because she is unwomanized by her education? Will the objector take the other horn of the dilemma and assert that she ought not to be educated? If so the logic must be pressed to its ultimatum. Either forbid women to learn the alphabet or concede all that a knowledge of the alphabet implies. Either repress and root out every tendency to mental growth and activity or prepare to accept the results when the mental faculties of women grow out into the full sunshine of eternal truth.

But let us go back to nature again; let us see if she does not suggest a solution to this problem. There was a period in our social development when this problem of finding rewarding activities for girls in the home did not give trouble. It was in the days of domestic manufactures. When women spun and wove and made linen and starch and soap and candles and cheese and the clothes both for themselves and the men of the family they really had stimulating, happifying and rewarding occupation. Why? Because the results of their labors were tangible. They were the outward and visible results of an inward living activity. It is often complained that our industrious grandmothers were far

happier and more contented than their luxurious
and cultivated granddaughters. So they were.
Well they might be. They found ready to their
hands rewarding, productive industries. In their
great rolls of cloth which their hands had spun and
woven, in their stacks of home-made blankets and
quilts, in the innumerable articles of use of domestic manufacture in their homes they had *something
to show*, and the inspiring correlative of their work
was tangible wealth.

Through no fault of women, but in consequence
of the working of the great central law of modern
civilization, the organization and division of labor,
and in consequence of the introduction and perfec-
tion of machinery, all domestic manufactures that
are productive have been removed from the home
to the manufactory. The occupations of the home
now, with the exception of the care of children,
consist mainly in repairing the ravages of daily
life. Woman no longer finds in the home the correlative of her powers and faculties in rewarding,
stimulating, wealth-producing work. Can she
adjust the balances of her life, can she find the
proper equilibration of her powers without it? Or
shall she go outside of the home to seek it? We
shall soon find that we are going in direct opposition to nature's laws if we accept inaction, stag-

nation or even mere occupation as the necessary alternative. By the unhappiness and ennui she inflicts, nature will do all she can to compel us to find another way. It will be a new phase of the old struggle of the organism with the environment.

What then is the impelling power that causes an educated womanhood everywhere to seek for more opportunities for the expression of educated faculties and for a greater share in the true work of the world? Why are women organizing in every little town and hamlet their clubs for social, literary and benevolent purposes? Why are they interesting themselves in school systems and benevolent institutions and asking that their work and influence may be utilized in the boards that control these institutions? Why are they seeking to obtain an independent share in the pecuniary interests of the world? Why, indeed, are they declaring that they want a voice in the choosing of law-makers, and also that women should have a share in administering the government? Why do they ask that every profession and every avocation of life be freely opened to them? It is because they feel the impulsion of that immutable law of growth which demands scope for development. The walls of the individual home can no more afford sufficient scope for action for the expanding and growing powers of women than the bulb can contain the hyacinth when it feels the impulse of the spring. It is not simply in order that they may be able to defend themselves against the necessities and the emergencies of life, that this wider scope for action is required; for it would not mend the matter or solve the problem were every educated woman fully defended pecuniarily from all the adversities of life. Woman's expanding powers would still demand for their satisfaction, work—*rewarding work*. This is still the insatiable demand of the immortal spirit as it expands and unfolds through intellectual development. Rewarding activity is the only content; it is the only condition in which is possible true repose of spirit.

Recognizing, then, the necessity that exists from the very nature of things that educated young women shall find worthy occupation for their time and talents,—not merely because a necessity exists or may some time be laid upon them to earn their own living; not merely because they are disposed to be "strong-minded," and to "think and feel like men" in the sense that Mrs. Orr means, but because their right relation to life demands scope for their intellectual energies and mental and bodily activities, and because their happiness requires work that commands some commensurate reward—the most important problem that presents itself to parents of the educated young women of to-day is that of suitable and satisfying and rewarding occupations for them. Society has already advanced far enough on this subject to recognize the fact that the parents of any young woman who during her school years develops a special talent for some of the higher forms of work, as literature, music, painting, or who feels drawn towards teaching in its higher departments as a congenial work, are fortunate. In our country at least it is most honorable for educated young women, the daughters of parents in comfortable or even wealthy circumstances, to devote themselves to remunerative work in any of these higher departments of labor. The problem of life is in the main solved for them, as it is for any human being when a congenial life-work is found. As Carlyle impressively says, "There is a perennial nobleness and even sacredness in work.... The whole soul of a man is composed into a kind of real harmony the instant he sets himself to work.... Destiny has on the whole no other way of cultivating us. A formless chaos, once set it *revolving*, grows round and even rounder, ranges itself by mere force of gravity into strata, spherical courses; is no longer chaos but a round compacted world." And again he says,

"Blessed is he who has found his work, let him ask no other blessedness.... Labour is life: from the inmost heart of the Worker rises his God-given Force, the sacred celestial Life-essence breathed into him by Almighty God; from his inmost heart awakens him to all nobleness,—to all knowledge, 'self-knowledge' and much else, so soon as work fitly begins." But even Carlyle failed to recognize the fact that this grand fundamental truth which he announced applied to women as well as men. * This is the truth that society is just waking up to perceive; this is the natural law whose manifestations are so perplexing and bewildering to thousands of good people of the present age and generation. To this law all normal, social and domestic life must and will yet adjust itself.

But outside of these higher occupations; outside of cases of exceptional talent and adaptability to special high pursuits, where are we to find scope for the activities of educated young women in the ordinary walks of life?

---

* Since this paper was written the publication of Carlyle's Reminiscences and of the Life and Letters of Mrs Carlyle have given the world an insight in to the heartworkings of that home which ought to have been one of the happiest, but was not. But how suggestive of one of the main causes of that unhappiness is this extract from one of Mrs. Carlyle's letters: "To be sure, it is hard on flesh and blood when one has nothing to keep one at home, to sit down in honest life-weariness and look out into unmitigated zero; but, perhaps, it would be a great advantage just to go ahead in that; the bare-.aced indigence of such a state might drive one, like the piper's cow, to 'consider,' and who knows but in considering long enough one might discover what one has wanted—an essential preliminary to getting it."

It would be well to digress a moment here to mark the strong emphasis which belongs to this question. Especially do I wish that I could gain the ear of fathers upon this point.   Men are so apt, in the pressure of business and their own affairs, to forget women.   They say, in a kind of general way, "Oh, we don't want women to work; it is our duty and pleasure to support them, and to guard them against the necessity of engaging in anything but domestic occupations.   Do let them be quiet and contented, and for heaven's sake let them be domestic.   We will *give* them everything they want if they will only not be progressive and strong-minded."   And then they go off to their daily occupations and engage in them with the zest that comes from remunerative work, and their educated daughters seek in vain for some mode of satisfactory expression for their cultivated faculties in the home.   There is no longer any rewarding occupation there.   There is no work to be accomplished, nothing to show as the worthy correlative of educated powers and cultivated, active minds.   Do men have any idea of the dreadful ennui that consumes thousands of well-educated, bright, aspiring girls in thousands of comfortable homes?   "What shall I do, papa?" was the weary question of one of these.   "Do, my dear! do—do? Well, suppose you do me a worsted dog on a pair of slippers." It is this lack of satisfying and productive occupation in the home, brought about by the inevitable progress of industrial organization, that has given rise to what a satirical writer has called the decorative art craze. If women could not do anything else that was satisfactory, they could at least decorate their homes. This is all very well as far as it goes, and if not carried too far; but many a house, with its wilderness of useless bric-a-brac, tidies, ornamented paper-holders and shoe-bags, embroidered rugs and stools, which men stumble over and then mutter words not meant for polite ears, is a pathetic appeal for something to do for the daughters of the household. "Something to do, something to do," is still the insatiable cry of the active, growing child, who, in uttering it, expresses one of the immutable laws of being. It is still the insatiable demand of the immortal spirit as it expands and unfolds through intellectual development.

Difficult as is at present the problem of suitable and remunerative employment for educated women, it is one that is constantly growing easier of solution because of the rapid changes which are taking place in the modes of domestic and social life owing to the wonderful effects wrought by the industrial organization of society. Hitherto it has been the fashion to insist upon, as of paramount importance, the domestic training of girls, but this has in a large measure lost its meaning since the organization of labor and the introduction of machinery has so nearly removed from the home all the arts of domestic production. And he is a superficial observer of the signs of the times who does not perceive that it will not be long until all the remaining domestic arts will follow those already departed out of the home. Even cooking will ere long become in cities and villages an outside organized industry just as laundry work and clothes-making have become. Institutions specially planned for the purpose will in the near future send us our appetizing ready-cooked meals promptly into our houses, and the perplexing servant question in the home will in the main be solved by the removal of all the unpleasant drudgery by outside industrial organization. We will then need in our homes only helpers in the care and training of our children, and these may be educated, refined, companionable young women.

In the almost entire removal of this general mass and muss of disorganized housework from our homes, one of the greatest difficulties in the way of specializing and thus rendering effective and remunerative the work of educated women will be removed. Every daughter in the home can feel free to select and follow some special occupation—in fact will feel that this is the proper thing to do just as do her brothers. What such occupations shall be, time will more fully develop. A great many pleasant and remunerative occupations are now open to women, and more will constantly open as girls more generally undertake to follow them and as the conditions of home and social life favor their entrance into them.

And in the outside organized work of the world all the lighter and more delicate departments of manufacturing will in time be given over to women; clerical work, the great departments of distributive production, including the selling of goods, book-keeping, etc., will more and more give employment to educated young women.* Here let me digress to say a word as to what I consider the true chivalry of the nineteenth century. We sometimes hear

---

* To those parents who shrink, as doubtless many do, at the thought of their daughters going out from the refined and protecting surroundings of the home to engage in wage-earning occupations there is encouragement in observing how the surroundings of labor, especially in the great departments of manufacturing and distributing production, are being improved and made even beautiful and elegant by our great commercial princes. In Boston, in New York, in Chicago, there are establishments where hundreds of girls and women are employed under such conditions and with such surroundings of convenience and elegance as ensure health and comfort. The increase of the number of great buildings specially planned for the admission of air and light, with elevators and fire-escapes, with appointments for the comfort of those employed in them as elegant as in first-class hotels, is one of the best signs of the approaching paradise of labor where our daughters shall follow special occupations under desirable conditions and with refined surroundings. Alas that for so many of the uneducated, uncared for classes of women-workers the exact reverse now obtains!

people sigh for the chivalric age when beautiful maidens lived in castles and their brave knights thought it their highest pleasure and honor to defend them from robbers and wild beasts and the shocks of war. That age has passed away; there are no longer great forests in which bandits and robbers and wild beasts prowl and hide. Woman's life and honor and happiness are no longer endangered by these; but they are endangered by subtler foes from which only her own hand can defend her. Lack of employment, lack of power, lack of opportunity, lack of education, a feeble physical development—these are the foes of womanhood in this age of the world. He is the true knight errant who says to woman: "Here is an easy place where you can earn independence and comfort; take it and I will get out and hunt me a harder place which you cannot fill." He is the truly chivalric man who says: "Here! there are thousands of refined and educated women who want remunerative work— who are endangered by lack of it.' Clear out these offices; remove those spittoons; carpet these floors; stop swearing and talking roughly; bring in these fair women and give them a chance—an equal chance with ourselves at the work of the world." And as for the man who in addition to all this says: "and we will give them equal pay for equal work," he is the noblest knight errant of them all, for he thus expresses and illustrates the noblest human virtue, Justice.

We will hope and expect however that our educated daughters, many of them, will open up new avenues for themselves and achieve great things. Here allow me to remark that I have as I believe arrived at a correct definition of a *feminine occupation*—or at least of what has hitherto been regarded by the world as a proper feminine occupation. It has been said that women cannot generalize—or rather that they generalize from one fact. As the result of one of my first attempts at generalization I would define a feminine occupation to be *one that is not organized and that has no money in it.* Take for instance washing and ironing! Although the very hardest kind of work with the very poorest kind of pay, so long as it is done by women singly and alone it is a strictly feminine occupation. Get up a steam laundry, organize the work and do it so as to make money by it and it becomes an honorable masculine occupation, and, as I have before remarked, in large cities laundry work is passing largely into the hands of men, where, doubtless, it properly belongs. Spinning and weaving were feminine occupations until the power loom was invented and cloth woven by the million yards, when it at once became an honorable and desirable masculine occupation, and not a woman ever thought to quote the bible to prove that women alone should use the distaff and spindle. So of soap-making, starch-making, cheese-making, candle-making, clothes-making—any occupation that women ever did engage in—just as soon as it can be so organized as to make money and evolve power it ceases to be a feminine occupation. I am sure a close scrutiny into this subject will prove that hitherto whatsoever things were weak, whatsoever things were small, whatsoever places or occupations were without power, or influence, or pay, or were disagreeable, have been considered *truly feminine.*

A woman who has achieved great things for herself has said that she receives a thousand letters every year from girls and women asking her what they shall do. She says she has but one reply for each and all, and that is "Thou alone canst answer." While we should endeavor to prepare the way by all means in our power for the recognition of our daughters as rightful co-laborers with our sons, and justly entitled to equal opportunities to earn and control their wages, yet let us remember that if our daughters would achieve great things, they must pay the price in struggle and anxiety.　Eschylus says that glories are the children of hardship and God's favor.　Our daughters must know that no one achieves great things without earnest, long sustained effort; that discouragements must be bravely encountered, defeats and disappointments accepted without allowing these to cause them to swerve from their course if they would accomplish great things.

When young women are thus prepared by a liberal education for lives of usefulness and self-support we shall expect the question of their marriage to be one which they shall be as free to decide as are our young men.　If for any reason they choose to remain single the title "old maid" will not have any stigma for them.　It is inevitable that the removal of any external pressure of necessity to marry for the sake of a home and a support will have a tendency to elevate the standard of marriage, first among women and then among men.　One of the greatest foes to happy marriages is the existence of the mercenary spirit on the part of parents and daughters.　Nothing will so effectively remove it as the possession by young girls and women of satisfactory, honorable, remunerative occupations, and the countenance and approbation of society in their pursuit of them.　We have now before us so many beautiful examples of single women who live happy,

useful and independent lives in charming homes of
their own, and who occupy the highest social position, that our educated daughters need not fear if
for any reason they choose in this respect to imi-
tate their example. Alice and Phoebe Cary, in their
beautiful home, once the center of one of the most
charming and cultivated social circles in the world,
Harriet Martineau, Jean Ingelow and others occur
to our minds as representatives of happy, honored
maiden life. Time would fail me to tell of Mary
Carpenter, Elizabeth Peabody, Florence Nightin-
gale, Caroline Herschel, Emily Faithful, Octavia
Hill, Maria Mitchell. These have all lived in faith,
and were persuaded that there is a high and holy call-
ing for women, even though they do not marry,—
are never wife and mother; and through faith and pa-
tience they have inherited the promise of old, that
to those who love truth and righteousness and follow on to know the Lord there shall be given a
name and place better than of sons and daughters.

It is a very encouraging sign of the times that
many parents who occupy high social position
and have abundance of means to maintain their
daughters in luxury and idleness, were they so disposed, are seriously considering the question of occupation for their daughters, and even taking practical steps towards securing it. I heard a wealthy bank-

er say, a short time since, that it was his intention as soon as his daughter graduated, to take her into the bank and have her thoroughly and practically instructed in bank business. I heard an eminent judge declare a very few weeks ago that his two daughters were to come into his law office on the completion of their school education, and learn to do office work. They were to be his clerks and amanuenses. I was further delighted to learn that in both cases these fathers expected to recognize the value of their daughters' services by paying them in money.

The prejudice against the earning of money by women, even among those fortunately situated in life, has measurably passed away, even as has passed away, or is passing away in the old world the prejudice against members of the nobility entering upon commercial avocations, and as is passing away the sentiment that condemned the artist or poet who asked pecuniary reward for the creations of his genius. Byron indignantly sent back a check to his publishers when at the same time there was an execution in his house for debt, but the poet Tennyson does not hesitate to make a good strong bargain for so many pounds a line for his poetry when negotiating with his publishers. And so we hope the day is about past when women who do anything to earn money must feel called upon to apologize

for it; when the comfortably situated housekeep-
er who has a few boarders must feel it incum-
bent on her to explain that she only takes them
for company; or when the woman who teaches
music must assert that she only does it for the sake
of keeping up her own knowledge of the science.
And above all we hope the day is near at hand
when it will not be considered a reflection on father, brother or husband, that daughter, sister or
wife does something that is rewarded in money·
For money is the most wonderful and delicate instrument of power that civilization has ever pro-
duced.   It is the agent by which we adjust ourselves to life; it is the universal solvent by which
we transmute our labor from any one form into any
other form.   It is the great emancipator.   When
labor ceased to work under the compulsion of the
lash and began to work for the incentive of pay,
the slave became the man.   In this liberty to handle
as he pleased the money he earned, the most inspiring of human motives was presented to him.
All toil, even the most monotonous and disagreeable,
is ennobled and dignified by the money which is its
reward.   The patient bricklayer, from early morn
till evening, with roughened hands and bended back
and grimy garments, picks up and lays down and
mortars his bricks, performing the same motions

endlessly over and over again.   What prevents
him or any other routine toiler from becoming a
mere callous human machine?   It is the thought
of the money which his work will bring by which
this hard, monotonous toil is transmuted into food
and raiment and shelter, into comfort and even
beauty for his wife and little ones.   This it is that
cultivates the best sentiments of humanity in his
heart, prevents him from becoming a clod, makes
a man of him.   And since the progress of womanhood is in the direction of the acquisition of knowledge, which is power; since the one inevitable result
of woman's education will be desire for the exercise of
power, the next stage of her progress will be to
learn the use and value of the power and influence
which comes through the possession of money—all
the more enjoyable if this money represents work
done by herself—power evolved by her own life
forces.

Thus far I have considered the future of educated women in the aspect of its relation to the individual only.   I have endeavored to elucidate the
true relation to life held by women who instead of
"filling spheres" are spheres themselves, revolving
on their own axes, performing their own orbits.
Life's fairest prospect for them, however, must ever
be that of honored and beloved wifehood and happy

motherhood.   What about their special occupations
then? I hear it asked.   I reply unhesitatingly that
in the case of a great many special occupations they
will probably have to cease while women are engaged
in the care of the infancy and youth of their children.
But that will not harm them.   It will only leave
room in the world of work for those who are coming on ready to fill their places.   They will also
be possessed of the happy consciousness that if
necessity requires they can return to their special occupations.   They will not be oppressed by
the fear that hangs like the sword of Damocles
over the heads of thousands of wives and mothers,
viz: that they may be deprived by death not only of
husband, but of home and support, and thrown
with their little ones helpless and dependent on
the cold charities of the world.

Several important advantages will result to educated women in married life from their practised
ability to earn money and fill important and rewarding positions in the world of work.   In the first place
husbands and society in general will come to have
a more just appreciation of the value—pecuniary
value if you like—of a wife's work in the care of
her home and rearing of her family.   The fact will be
better appreciated that when an intelligent, capable
labor-competent woman resigns all opportunities for

earning money, and thus independence and comfort for herself, to devote all her powers and risk health and even life itself for the sake of husband and children, some commensurate recognition of this sacrifice should be made in the partnership of the home.   The old fashioned idea that a wife is a dependent, is supported, will give away to the more just proposition that a wife should be regarded as partner entitled to the recognition of her services by sharing with her husband the control of his income.   Here I know I touch upon a delicate and difficult subject, but I do not hesitate to take the responsibility of declaring that this matter of the purse has been in times past, is now, in thousands of otherwise happy homes, the source of more unhappiness than good men have ever dreamed of.   I cannot explain my meaning in any way so well as by drawing for you from life two pictures of two educated women, asking which you shall choose as the fairer.

Both women are young, beautiful, educated talented, brilliant—the pride of their husbands. Both are mistresses of large establishments and keep numerous servants, a carriage, etc.   Both are the mothers of three little children.   One husband tells his wife to get everything she wants for the house and herself and the children and have

the bills sent to him monthly, and he never com-
plains no matter how large they are.   He keeps his
wife supplied with a fairly generous amount of general expense money, as he calls it, and occasionally
gives her besides twenty dollars, fifty dollars or even
in a special fit of generosity one hundred dollars.
But everything which she gets in money comes as a
gift from him; it is by no means accorded to her as
a recognition of the faithful work she performs
in the conducting of their home, or of the fact that
she has all the care of their children.   Now
this beautiful woman whose every want is
supplied, feels that she works just as hard,
expends just as much strength and vitality,
exercises her brain forces just as much in the care
of their home and children as her husband does in
his office.   In fact in this case she expends much
more vitality, for his business is organized and
runs smoothly, while hers is disorganized and runs
joltingly.   Before her marriage as a very superior
musician she earned and controlled a salary of two
thousand dollars a year.   She has friends near and
dear who are poor.   She has a widowed mother living
in comparative poverty; she has a young brother
struggling through college; she has a young sister with wonderful artistic tastes who needs assist-
ance in developing them in the shape of opportuni-

ty to study under good masters; yet this sister who is the wife of a rich man can do nothing for them except she places both herself and her friends in the light of beneficiaries of her husband. So very often she sits in her sumptuous parlors, twisting the diamond rings on her fingers, and groans in spirit to think that out of her husband's thousands she cannot control or call her own five hundred dollars. To be sure if she should *ask* him for money for herself or to assist her mother or brother he would probably give it—*give it!* He would be the benefactor and they the beneficiaries. .Often is the determination more .than half taken to again secure music pupils and have the proceeds of her labor for her very own to handle and do with as she pleases.

The other husband out of a generous income places a certain amount to his wife's credit in bank every month. When she has accumulated a considerable amount—as she often does—he advises her how to invest it in this direction and that. She buys bank and railroad stock; she owns two or three houses and collects the rent. She knows all about notes and drafts and checks and mortgages, and can calculate interest or discount. She can subscribe five hundred dollars to a church or an orphan aslyum; she can lend a struggling young girl or a widowed friend a few hundred dollars. She has none of that wretched feeling of being regarded as a dependent which is such a blight to the lives of thousands of married women. She feels that her labors in the sacred partnership of the home are recognized in a tangible way, hence has none of that feeling that so many housekeepers have that they spend their strength in vain and that their labor is for naught. And no one enjoys this state of things more than her husband. He often says that it is a source of constant satisfaction to him that his wife has such a knowledge of business that if he were called suddenly away he would not fear but that she could manage all their property interests. No trustees are needed to manage her property (away from her) and the knowledge of this fact is health to the heart of both husband and wife.

My second picture illustrates the probable effect of education on the married lives of our daughters when as wives and mothers they give up their whole time to the care of their homes and children. As the majority of homes are now organized this almost entire devotion of the wife's energies to the conduct of the home seems necessary. It is in every case a question of individual circumstances and disposition whether the wife shall have any other occupa-

tion. Certain it is, also, that it must be laid down as
an axiom around which all true social life shall re-
volve that a mother's first duty is to her children.
That is, and will always be, an abnormal condition of
society which brings a pressure to bear upon mothers to force them into money-making occupations
when their time is needed by their families and
homes. Nevertheless it is my opinion that as a
result of the organization of domestic labor by
which the most of the work of the home except
the care of children, will be taken out of the house
in cities or villages, the time is near at hand when
thousands of educated married women will aim to
have some specialty which they may still pursue
in their homes both as a satisfaction of their powers and as a means of earning money.

In homes of limited incomes I think the introduction of special work for the wives and mothers would
prove a great blessing. In defence of this opinion
I offer this simple illustration. We all know that
the wife of a man in moderate or limited circumstances, if she have a house and family, does a great
deal of work, and very hard work, too, besides taking care of her children. She cooks, she sweeps,
she bakes, she sews. In fact there is no more
common fallacy than to suppose that women who
are so "very domestic" as we phrase it, give unusual

care to their children; they do not,—they have not
the time.   Their energies are mainly taxed to get
the household work out of the way; to have
breakfast, dinner and supper promptly on the
table;—and to their children it is—"Oh run away"
—"do go off"—"do keep from under my feet;"
and happy are you, my friends, if in homes of re
spectability you have never seen little children
die really of neglect while the busy mother's over-
taxed energies were all absorbed in keeping up
with the exacting routine of housework.   I have
seen a little sick child, who should have had every
moment of its mother's attention and all her fresh-
est and best energies, left lying in its cradle while
she, poor woman, swept and cooked and worked;
and I have heard her wild anguish over its little
body when the frail life departed for want of the
necessary care to save it.   Well, I will suppose the
case of the mother of a family where the husband's
income is so limited that the wife feels that she
must do all her own work including the washing
and ironing.   To get her washing and ironing done
—taken clear away from the house,—will cost, say,
two dollars a week.   Now suppose this woman was
an expert, say on a sewing machine or a knitting
machine, or in some kind of special work that
would command pay.   Suppose that with her

house in order, her children playing about her, she sits down for two or three hours a day to this special work. If she did no more than pay the money she earned for the laundry work she hired done, who would say that this was not the better way? But it is probable she would earn considerably more.

This is only an illustration of a general principle in regard to the work of women in the home which must eventually be generally recognized in the progress of education and of the organization of labor. At the outset, however, one of the difficulties to be met and overcome is the feeling on the part of many husbands that they do not want their wives to work—for money. Now this is a feeling that has its root in a right sentiment, and I greatly respect it, although I think that with changing social conditions we need also to change our opinions and to beware of being governed by mere prejudice. It is a right and noble instinct that makes every true man feel that he must and ought to be the bread-winner for his family. Nevertheless no man objects but rather prides himself on the fact if he has an industrious, capable wife. If so, the question simply becomes a choice of work. A man who goes off to his work in the morning to remain away till noon, and then till night, has no reason for feeling happier if he knows that his wife in his absence is doing some hard household work in order to save money, rather than some easy special work for which she receives money in return. I have heard men boast of their wives' culinary exploits; I have seen them point with pride to the immense household tasks of which they were capable; I have experienced far more satisfaction when a gentleman in whose family I visited, showed me with pride and pleasure the beautiful panel pictures his wife painted and for which she received ten dollars apiece, the occupation affording her both delight and pecuniary reward. I have felt a real happy inspiration in looking over a large variety of wood carvings done by a delicate wife, whose husband also took pride and delight in her work, such as I never experienced in contemplating an elaborate meal cooked by an intelligent woman; and I have said: all of these things are tokens of an advancing civilization.

This principle holds good and becomes more and more apparent as we rise from the less educated to the more cultivated, capable and refined women of our land. When we reach the class who are not forced by necessity to endeavor to make their labor productive we reach those who are impelled by the inward forces, of which I spoke in the early part of my paper, to do something, to accomplish something, that shall worthily correspond to their educated powers and faculties. Here I trust I shall be pardoned for particularizing somewhat. For many years, first as teacher in a large seminary and afterwards in editorial work, I have been in a position to learn much of the aspirations, the efforts, the difficulties of educated women. I believe if it were generally known how many educated women, married and unmarried, are now seeking for opportunities to apply their cultivated powers to some work that would in return bring money, or in some way show a tangible, practical result, all would agree with me that such a general want indicates that a general remedy must be near at hand. On this point I speak authoritatively, for I speak what I know from personal experience and observation. I am sometimes surprised to find how strong is the desire to do something to earn money or to accomplish some pecuniary object even among the wealthy,---those from whom one might suppose the idea would be the farthest possible. A short time since a lovely gray-haired woman, the mother of a family of sons, showed me some poems and essays she had written, and when I expressed pleasure at their excellence and told her I thought she could get pay for them from standard magazines, she said: "Do you think so? oh, I think it would be so delightful to earn a little money." I may say that she sent the poems where I advised and received a check in return which seemed to delight her exceedingly. I know a very accomplished and elegant lady, the daughter of one senator and the wife of another, who has written a very successful cook-book. It is said her income from the royalty is about two thousand dollars a year, and many are the expressions that fall from the lips of her lady friends of "How fortunate she is!" "How she must enjoy having an independent income of her own!" "I wish I could write a cook-book," etc. Let no one condemn women, and let not women condemn themselves, for their earnest longings to realize worthy proportional results for their labors. Let them not be condemned for looking beyond the walls of the home to find opportunity for securing these results. This is not mere irrational discontent; rather it is the effort of growth. The unrest and disquietude of spirit that is so often coincident with such effort are a kind of spiritual growing pains which will pass away when that which fetters growth is removed. No feeling is more normal, more commendable than that which impels us to seek to effect results in some degree commensurate with our powers, and to feel dissatisfied and unhappy when we fail to do so.

I well remember the deep impression made upon my mind many years ago by listening to the conversation of a highly educated and highly gifted woman who had been a successful teacher before her marriage, as she half humorously, half pathetically detailed some of the experiences of her early married life. What she said was in effect this: "When my husband and myself settled down in our cozy little home after marriage the question of how I should occupy my time was a grave one. At first I undertook to do my own work. I observed that to get our little breakfast, wash the dishes and put my house in order took about four hours of my time. An equal amount of time spent in teaching before my marriage earned for me seventy-five dollars a month. I observed that to secure the result of three loaves of good bread my attention was kept on the stretch for about twelve hours. Accustomed before my marriage to methodical work and large results, the consciousness of spending such an amount of time and energy every day simply in getting three meals for two people really caused the most distressing sense of wasted and misdirected effort. I began to fear my teaching had rendered me undomestic in my tastes, and yet I loved my husband

and my home. I finally solved ·the problem, by hiring my housework done by a woman ,with more muscle and less brains than myself, who was excessively glad to get the work and the three dollars a week I paid her for it, while I betook myself to teaching private classes in literature, occupying myself just as I had done before marriage, earning thereby a handsome income. I was far happier in doing so and my home suffered no loss in consequence. Even after my children came I found that I was better in heart and richer in pocket for continuing my teaching, which was both a diversion from too constant household care and a source of personal income which was most enjoyable."

I have said that such a general social want indicates that a general remedy must be at hand. In nature and in the divine economy (which some call evolution) we see this constant provision for the newly developing needs of the human race. New articles of food, new methods of communication and transportation are constantly being discovered as humanity needs them. Years ago great alarm was expressed because it was discovered that the whale fisheries would not much longer be able to supply the demand for oil for light; yet before the whale fisheries were exhausted we had discovered rivers of oil in the depths of the

earth. England is occasionally agitated by the dec-
laration of scientists that it is but a question of
time till her coal-fields are exhausted; but before
the coals are exhausted, scientists have told us that
we shall get both heat and light from
electricity, and we are probably about to realize
this prediction. As the populations of the old
world have become too dense, ocean steamers and
trans-continental railways have multiplied so as to
meet the necessities of the people by bringing them
to the great fertile fields of the new world. So in
society. Since there is a necessity that women engage in other work than simply the care of children, and since in the rapid progress of industrial
organization it is evident that no other work will
much longer be distinctively the work of the home,
it is evident that we are tending to such a change
in social conditions as shall give to women generally an opportunity to share in the work and wages
of the world, in their homes if necessary, or by a
different arrangement of home life permitting them
to leave their homes for a portion of every day to
engage in remunerative labor.

And this change but presages other vital, rapidly
approaching changes. Educate women and they
will wish to exercise their cultivated powers in a
way that will produce a commensurate result. The

readiest form which that result will take will more
and more be money. The control of money gives
power. Power is sweet to every human heart.
Once exercised it is never willingly relinquished by
any human being. Women will learn the value of
money and of the power which its possession gives
and will naturally wish to learn to take care of it.
This will lead them into a new domain of thought
and experience, for it will make them practical and
intelligent participants in the social economy.

Property rights are great educators. Women
who are as unable to see the connection between
individual welfare and the law making power—in
other words the ballot—as the common sailor is to
understand the relation between compass and chro-
nometer and the movements of the stars—women
who are unaffected by any logic of argument are
very quickly taught by the logic of experience the
vital connection there is between self protection
on the part of property owners and the possession
of that little instrument which makes or unmakes
legislators. Women who feel the grasp of taxation,
or who personally experience the hurt of some un-
fair law, are at once led to ask the questions: Who
make the laws and to whom are lawmakers respon-
sible? Since my money helps pay the taxes, since
my property is disposed of by the law, I want a

voice in saying what shall be done with the taxes, and in saying who shall make laws to govern me." This of course is primarily a selfish interest in the law making power, but it is the first interest that will be taken by the awakening mind because it lies so near the individual and its connection is so apparent.* I have known women, who scouted the idea of wanting the ballot, very quickly converted to an exactly opposite opinion when the question of grading streets through their property, or of building a new school-house in their ward brought the relation directly home to them.

It takes a higher order of comprehension, a higher interest than personal selfishness to make women realize and wish for the power to help in forming social institutions through a voice in making the laws that create and govern them. That woman's mental and moral nature is developed to some purpose who, following her children out from the hearthstone into life, longs for the power to help mould the social conditions that surround them. What if the mother-heart yearns over the neglected children on the streets; over the young men who are tempted into saloons; over the

* In his essay on "The Progress of Culture" Emerson says: "Observe the marked ethical quality of the innovations urged or adopted. The very claim of woman to a political status is itself an honorable testimony to the civilization which has given her a civil status new in history. Now that by the increased humanity of law she controls her property she inevitably takes the next step to her share in power."

crowds of young girls who labor under the most
unhealthful conditions; over the suffering and forgotten inmates of hospitals and insane asylums;
over the still more sadly forgotten inmates of
houses of correction and prisons; what if she feels
that there ought to be more of the public money
spent for educational and eleemosynary institutions
so that less would be required for the care of the
criminal classes? That woman is educated to some
purpose who observing and thinking on these things
perceives that the way to render effective all these
hopes and wishes for the good of humanity is to
materialize them into effectiveness through the
possession of that wonderful and delicate instrument
of power which organizes social institutions, which
makes or unmakes laws, and which is even more ir-
resistible than the power of money. Here indeed is a
field of action for noble women in which they will
find a satisfaction in the good accomplished for humanity far beyond that of any material reward.
The highest activity of which humanity is capable and that which brings the richest reward
is that of being co-worker with the Divine in making better the conditions of human life. And these
conditions are made better or worse by human
agency through the exercise of that highest power,
the power to help make and administer the laws.

Here will finally be found the noblest field of action for educated women. Men are the most natural, the most efficient money-makers of the world; women are the most natural the most efficient caretakers of society. Education and freedom of action for women; the finding of activities which shall worthily correspond to their faculties will eventually give us the highest possible conditions of organized social life. Fair is the prospect for the future of educated women. Youth and maidenhood will be a period of happy, useful, rewarding activity; marriage will be elevated to that high plane where husband and wife shall each delight in the other because both delight in the eternal laws. The cares of maternity fulfilled, sons and daughters having gone out into life for themselves, the richest, the most useful period of the life of the educated woman begins. I have only suggested its possibilities. Shall I close with this little word to my sisters, from the universal poet, Goethe?

"Heard are the voices,
Heard are the sages,
The worlds and the ages,
'Choose well, your choice is
Brief but yet endless;

Here eyes do regard you
In eternity's stillness;
Here is all fulness,
Ye brave, to reward you.
Work and despair not.'"

Men, Women and Money.

Theseus: My country shall be thine, and there thy state regal.

Hippolyta: Am I a child? Give me my own and keep for weaker heads thy diadems. —Landor.

In his Spirit of the Laws Montesquieu says "The possessor of property is ever possessed of power." The truth would pass undisputed without high authority.

Probably one of the very strongest forces in the world's history is money.

A contempt for money is no part of the philosophy of modern society, nor has it ever really been of any society since civilization began. As stored energy, as a tangible and convertible result of labor, it is an ever present force, and it were as sensible to entertain a contempt for electricity as for money.

While the interests of men and women are so closely interwoven that they might be considered as the warp and woof of which society is the fin-

53

inished web, and while it is a futile reasoning which attempts to treat them as separate races with opposing interests, yet their relation to money has become so individual and personal that in considering it we must necessarily inspect the individual strands composing the fabric.

A glance at the world's history shows the co-incidence of the diffusion of power with the diffusion of property, from the time when all wealth was vested in the king, and his subjects were also his property,—down through the tribal and patriarchal systems and the varying stages of property rights of the heads of families to the present state of sole and individual property rights of men. But for lack of money kings would have ruled forever; and the degree in which men have been able to wrest from them the right to control money has measured the power which men individually and collectively could control.

Hitherto men have been, and to an overwhelming extent still are the earners of money, the bread-winners of the world, and consequently the possessors of its wealth, while women have been the dependent disbursers and exhibitors of that wealth. Comte says: "That man should provide for woman is a law of the human race; a law connected essentially with the domestic character of woman."

Everywhere men toil for money. In grimy mills, in dingy shops and offices, in dark mines, under burning suns, on the broad prairies, on the high seas, in crowded cities, in the marts of trade, in the bank parlors, in the counting rooms, on the wharfs, on the streets, are the anxious throngs of men toil-ing for money; and if some woman, more often two or three, as wife, daughter, mother, is not shar-ing the gold he earns the man is not a representa-tive man; it is largely true of the man of the pres-ent generation that the heart has gone from his work if there is no woman on whom he can spend the money he has earned.

Standing on one of the great thoroughfares of a great city at the hour in the evening when the day's work is over and the crowds of laborers are returning to their homes it will be an impressive thought, as it is an undoubted fact, that of all this toiling throng of men ninety-nine out of every hundred have been working all day long for some woman and her children. Somewhere is a home which he as a man maintains, and in it a woman more or less attached to him on whose needs he will expend the greater part of what he has earned by the sweat of his brow.

Not that we fail to note also the living stream of weary women, young and old, shop girls and sewing

women, scrubbing women and drudges of every
description returning from their day's work; but
these women do not represent the great earning
power and fortune making forces of society; many
of them do not earn as much in a week as a labor-
ing man in a day; they keep from starving, and at
the best eke out a bare living, but they do not accumulate a competence, or ever even dream of a fortune. If in a year from now one of these women is in
better circumstances in life, with more comforts and
more money to spend, it will not, in nine cases out
of ten, be the result of her own exertions, but because some man has commenced to earn her living
for her.   Not that woman has not also been the in-
heritor of the curse of toil with her brother; she
has equally the curse, but has not yet inherited with
him the reward of that toil.

Looking at all the departments of the world's
work where money is earned, it seems to be a world
of men.   But looking where money is spent the
actors change and we see a world of women.

Everywhere, in the crowds of pleasure seekers at
home and abroad, women largely predominate with
men enough along to do all the hard work. Women
fill our excursion steamers on the great lakes, float
down the broad rivers and swarm at noted pleasure
resorts; they are the special patrons at home and

abroad of theatres, concerts and operas. They fill our great city dry goods palaces and jewelry stores, and all kinds of stores in smaller towns. Everywhere that money can buy luxuries, comforts, necessaries, there you find woman at her post diligently doing her duty, spending for man the money he has earned.

This has been the ancient and hereditary relation of woman to money since she rose from the condition of being a chattel herself. Nor could it be otherwise in a less advanced stage of civilization than the one which is presently dawning upon us. A shuddering glance backward through the world's history at woman's relation to society shows that relation to have been solely maternal in the baldest, most physical sense so long as man's relation to it was mostly warlike. The men whom she agonized to bear strew the world's battle-fields; and woman, when she did not share with them the horrid fortunes of war, wept unheeded over her children slain.

The climax of man's brutality and woman's helplessness is recorded in the words of Napoleon to a woman so late as the beginning of this century, when his bloody wars had swept from France all the flower of her manhood, and the conscription was hurrying away to fresh slaughter regiments composed of youths of seventeen: "Madame" said this only recently unmasked monster, "what France needs to-day, is mothers." So long as war was the business of mankind it necessarily followed that woman's place in the world was a subordinate and degraded one; but after the fall of the Roman Empire came the establishment of the feudal system which determined the condition of society in which originated any permanent property rights and, through them, any stable power for women.

Man has ever had a tender heart towards his daughter, and in such fashion as he could endeavored to protect her from gross harm in a world where he well knew the law of the strongest prevailed, and property in land for women in the form of dower-right was speedily engrafted on the feudal system. It is more than a coincidence that the age of chivalry soon followed and woman acquired an additional charm in the eyes of her lover. This acquisition of property rights was a great stride in the advancement of women to a more equal place in the society of men.

.John Stuart Mill, in his exhaustive essay on the subjection of women, distinctly states that "through all the progressive periods of human history the condition of women has been approaching nearer equality with men;" yet he touches but

lightly on the advancing property rights and pecuniary independence of women as an elevating
power, because, as he says, "institutions, books,
education, society, all go on training human beings
for the old long after the new has come, much
more when it is just coming;" he thus almost
laughably illustrates his own reiterated statement
of the impossibility of any man knowing what any
woman really thinks on most vital questions. It is
more than probable the wife of John Stuart Mill,
idolized as she was by her husband, never told him
how much she hated to ask him for a five pound
note.

The money independence of woman has been an
almost unnoted force in her elevation to anything
like equal power in the world, but it is one which
must precede her possession of political power as
surely as the blade precedes the full corn in the
ear.

The possibility of the development of the earning
power of woman has only just dawned; but the
alphabet of the new and higher knowledge has been
learned and full education must inevitably follow.

It is scarcely three generations since women,
with very rare exceptions, have even begun
to try their capacity in the quiet and easily accessi-
ble fields of the intellectual world, and it is only in

the present generation that women have developed
an extreme longing for independence in their relations to money. It is in this generation that woman stretches out her hand towards labor and its rewards.   Finding that custom and the usages of
society have barred her from multitudes of avenues
of money-making enterprises, and lack of education
and training from many others, she has crowded
those where she might enter to the point of suffo-
cation.

It is a pitiful sight to the lover of humanity to
look at the records of labor during the last century,
the painful conditions of which still endure and
must endure for some time yet. Thousands of weary,
half-starved women have impaled their lives on the
point of the needle. Nor has the modern sewing
machine improved their condition.

The great army of women teachers we now have
always with us, whose ranks are constantly crowded
with new recruits. The legions of shop-women come
and go on our streets. Many women are knocking
at the forbidding looking doors of the professions
with varying success, and thousands strive to eke
out a living with the pen.

Underlying all this effort is the one constant and
imperious longing not only for the wherewithal to
sustain life but also for the expression of the fun-

damental necessity in the lives of the cultivated and educated for pecuniary independence; while at the same time the actual condition of things has passed into the proverb, "Men make fortunes, women make livings."

Individual property and the tangible reward in dollars and cents for the work of her hands and her brains has come to be the universal desire of the better and more highly educated class of women; and although the office of prophet is a cheap one, and with little honor, it may safely be assumed long enough to say that undoubtedly the superior woman of the future will not be supported.

This desire of woman for independence in money matters is but a natural development of her advancing position in society from a dependent and inferior state of childhood and tutelage towards the full stature of womanhood and equality with her brother. It is a state from which he too has formerly emerged, and unless woman is to remain in the world of achievement where Darwin has placed her in the physical, " an arrested development," she must aspire to this independent position.

Concerning the unmarried woman, the echo of the question, "Is she obliged to?"—meaning, "Can not her father or her brother support her?"—is still in the ears of this generation; and her mother still thinks it necessary to say, "She don't work for the money but for the pleasure of doing the work." All of which is only pitiful nonsense! The pleasure of earning, possessing and controlling money is one which every thinking woman has long envied her brother; and that she should aspire to it as soon as possessed of full education follows as surely as effect follows cause.

In this country, in any considerable community, may be counted many men, from the millionaire down to the man with a competence, who have with their own hands and brains and without inherited means made their fortunes; but the only rich women are the wives of such men, rich by courtesy, or the widows and daughters whose husbands and fathers dying left them wealth. A woman who has herself made a fortune is a *rara avis* in any community, although the women who support themselves are legion.

Self-support is of course the first step on the way to competence, and the multitude of women, like the multitude of men, will never reach a higher plane; but there are women who will undoubtedly turn their attention to the accumulation of money; who will themselves strive for a home and a competence, and dream of a fortune.

No woman who has read Harriet Martineau's description of the joy and satisfaction with which she took possession of her house and her field, earned by herself, but has felt a stirring of the pulses at the achievement, an answering thrill and a wish to do likewise.

The home which the Cary sisters made for themselves, and from which they shed the steady light of their gentle influence, shines as a star among the traditions of literary New York.

Despite the modern multiplication of boarding houses I cannot but believe that the love of a home is inherent in woman's nature, and as inseparable from it as the instinct of nest building from the nature of birds.

And truly a woman advanced in life, without a home and occupation, is a picture without a frame, a barren fact which is lacking in the dignity of fit surrounding circumstances. A home of her own is what every woman craves whose original impulses are not vitiated by false aims. If there is a husband in it, —ah! delightful! but any way, at all events, a home.

In the vast and ever advancing organization of industries, which is one of the phenomena of modern life, homes must come to be more and more delightful places, and the lighter and less cumbrous tasks must fall to feminine hands. Whether women

can ever in great numbers earn more than a bare
living remains to be seen; but the desirableness of
such a state of things cannot be questioned. It is
undoubtedly true that the unknown quantity in
every woman's life is marriage; not only in youth
but up to middle life. It is this which stands as a
barrier between her and every occupation for which
years of training are required. Lawyers do not
want clerks who may only half learn the profession.
Telegraph operators find it a serious objection to
teaching a girl that she may marry before she has
completed her apprenticeship; and so on through
all the trades and occupations in which men succeed;
in fact a woman only seems to increase her chances
for marriage by going out into the world to make a
living because of the closer and more frequent relation in which it throws her with men. Observation seems to show that as soon as a girl can make
a living for herself she is almost sure to marry.
Aside from other considerations marriage has been
the shortest way to a competence and other desirable conditions for women.

Disraeli, in his novel of Endymion, makes one of
his young men wish that he were a woman in order
that he might cut short the weary struggles for advancement in the world. Speaking of the years of
toil which a man starting with nothing must give

to gain an advanced position in life he contrasts them with the lot of a woman in similar circumstances who may meet a fortune and position in the drawing room, sit next it once or twice at dinner and the next month possess it by marriage.

It is impossible that ever such a state of society should exist that it would be better on the whole for a woman's happiness for her to remain unmarried. It is true to-day as it always has been that no better lot can come to a woman than has come if a good man has loved her and she has married him.

And now the fact that the great majority of women are and will always be married women brings us to a consideration more especially of the present relation of married women to property.

Without entering into the entangling details of the laws in relation to married women and property it is sufficient for our purpose to state that broadly speaking, they are at present in most of our states in favor of the wife in the event of the death of her husband or her divorce from the marriage relation. But during her married life she occupies the same position towards her husband's property as her children.

Most married women's ideas are in a state of chaos on the subject of money and property rights.

Marrying young, usually at an age when men

could not have made any start in the direction of a
competence, they are generally dazzled with the
silly notion that all that is their husband's is theirs;
which is a most false and pernicious idea of which
every thinking woman should speedily divest herself;
for money is no more a condition of the atmosphere
between two people because they are married than
it is in the outside world. It is in fact a most individual entity, and resides with one or the other of
the parties to the contra.

Examined into she will find that, beyond purely
personal expenditures, her property is by all law,
custom and usage purely one of expectation; a
doleful waiting for "dead men's shoes," a property
of which it is a treachery to a beloved husband
even so much as to think; and by which, so far as
present control avails, she might as well try to en-
rich herself as by reading over the accounts of for-
eign specie imports. She will find herself con-
fronted with the perplexing paradox, that she *has*
only what money she spends, and if she saves it she
don't have it. Most men resent the wish in their
wives to have a separate purse or individual accumulation of property as a reflection on themselves,
though this feeling is unreasonable and entirely
one of education and tradition.

As culture advances this position of married

women toward the purse becomes more and more
irksome.   Admitting that in the ideally perfect
marriage the question of money is no question,
yet, as a wide observer of married life has said,
most marriages are fragmentary, and since it is so
it is idle to expect ideal results from imperfect conditions.   In this direction of the money question
lies a vast, undiscovered domain of sensitive and
refined misery among otherwise happily married
women.

Montesquieu says: "The community of goods....
between husband and wife is extremely well
adapted to a monarchical government because
women are thereby interested in domestic affairs and
compelled as it were to take care of their families.
It is less so in a republic.....As women are in a
state that furnishes sufficient inducements to them
to enter into marriage the advantages which the
laws give them over the property of their husbands
are of no service to society." This was written
nearly three centuries ago and the "sufficient in-
ducement" then was woman's extreme defenseless-
ness. It is evident the philosopher never contemplated a state of society in which women would be
possessed of independent property within the marriage relation, and consequently possessed of that
power which he said always belongs to property, any

more than he contemplated the existence of such a
repub'ic as the United States when he says "it is
impossible republics can long exist except they be
very small."

The making of a home and the maternal functions do not absorb all the energies of married women except during a portion of their lives, but
hitherto there has been no present money value
to the office of motherhood; and the business of
housekeeping, beyond a maintenance, is one of the
unremunerative industries.

Yet mankind has ever extolled the office of the
wife and mother and home maker, placing her services beyond price, and doubtless it is this exagger-
ated estimate which has silenced her when she
would ask for her own; but women would be much
happier to accept a lower estimate for the sake of
a more tangible reward.

A man takes care that his wife shall have her
own when he is no longer able to protect her, and,
as before stated, in the event of the death of her
husband the law runs in favor of the wife; but
dower and many life insurance policies simply
represent the accumulated and unpaid wages of
married women; property which comes to her from
the hand of death which she should have enjoyed
during her husband's life-time; that which he should

have helped her to accumulate and manage as her own property, and to enter into which would require no process of law and ministry of sorrow.

Take an ordinary case of two young people commencing life with a modest sum. Let years and prosperity follow: at forty the husband has a home, wife, children, an income, and property; his wife, with the exception of the children and richer personal surroundings, is no better off than she was twenty years ago; controls no more money, still spends what her husband gives her, and is generally extremely ignorant on the subject of the proper management of property. She is also in the uncomfortable position of a person who spends personally, and on whom is spent, the most money, but who has none to command. It is the position of a child and a minor from which the husband, the children and the home life all suffer.

As such a woman goes on toward middle life and old age the circumstances are more and more depressing, resulting generally in a narrowing of her whole nature and a painful repression of her best impulses.

Any changes for the better in this condition of things must come, first from a changed mode of thinking on the part of married women themselves on the subject of property, and then from concessions to that change on the part of men.

Married women must divest themselves of the childish notion that their husband's property is their own. That is not property which one does not control, and it needs only a little thinking to convince a woman that only in the event of her husband's death does she really own the vaunted and traditional "one third."

Let her calmly take stock and enquire, "What property have I? What do I earn? What is so indisputably my own that without any shadow of wronging my husband, I might, if I saw fit, with dignity bestow alms upon the beggar whom he dislikes?" If she finds herself without either money or goods, she will at least be a step in advance of the fallacy of supposing she has something when she has nothing.

Mill, speaking on a kindred subject, says: "There are no doubt women, as there are men, whom equality of consideration will not satisfy; with whom there is no peace while any will or wish is regarded but their own. Such persons are proper subjects for divorce. They are fit only to live alone, and no human beings ought to be compelled to associate their lives with them. But legal subordination tends to make such characters among women more rather than less frequent. If the man exerts his whole power the woman is of course crushed; but if she is treated with indulgence and permitted to assume power there is no rule to set limits to her encroachments. The law not determining her rights, but theoretically allowing her none, practically declares that the measure of what she has a right to is what she can contrive to get."

This reasoning is particularly applicable to the spending of money by married women; the amount of embarrassment a silly and unscrupulous woman can cause her husband is incalculable.

A woman who had nothing when she married, and whose services to the married partnership have not been worth her maintenance, can, if she choose, embarrass a fortune which she neither earned nor inherited, and to which she has no just claim.

It is a case of privileges without corresponding obligations, and should give way to the individual and independent ownership of property among cultivated and refined people.

Mill further says: "When the support of the family depends not on property but on earnings, the common arrangement by which the man earns the income and the wife superintends the domestic expenditures seems to me in general the most suitable division of labor between two persons."

This is quite true, but there should be a money

value to both sides in the division of labor, and
that belonging to the making of a home should be
paid, not to the man, but to the woman individually.

"In an otherwise just state of things," says the
same writer, "it is not a desirable custom that the
wife should contribute by her labor to the income of
the family, though the power of earning is essential to the dignity of a woman if she have not independence and property."

But if her labor as the maker of a home receive
from the family income its just and due reward in
present possessions without waiting for the hand of
death to deal out to her a just portion, the making
of homes would rise to the highest point in the
scale of occupations for women.

The best interests of society demand that this
change shall speedily be brought about.

Marriage with the advent of children, while it
can never be to woman the episode merely which
it is to a man in his life-work, yet by no means occupies more than a part of her life; and as "there is
nothing after disease, indigence and guilt so fatal to
the pleasurable enjoyment of life as a want of a
worthy outlet for the active faculties," so to most
women, as to most men, the management of individual property interests would furnish this outlet.

"There are abundant examples of men who, after a life engrossed by business, retire with a competency to the enjoyment, as they hope, of rest; but to whom, as they are unable to acquire new interests to replace the old, the change to a life of inactivity brings ennui, melancholy and premature death. Yet no one thinks of the parallel case of so many worthy and devoted women who, having paid their debt to society—having brought up a family blamelessly to manhood and womanhood, having kept house as long as they had a house needing to be kept—are deserted by the sole occupation for which they had fitted themselves and remain with undiminished activity, but with no employment for it."

As I said before, woman must work out the solution of this problem herself. No laws, no legislation can help her.

A woman who is making a home and rearing children does her position great injustice in allowing herself for a moment to think she is supported.

Beside the sentimental and affectionate partnership in marriage there should be a money partnership which should plainly state her individual financial condition, and both husband and wife should regard with favor the accumulation of her individual and separate property side by side with his, though perhaps and necessarily much smaller. True, there would be more accounts kept, but there would be more solid happiness.

If in the course of time the earning power of woman shall approximate more nearly that of man, and she can engraft on the occupation of marriage and maternity one which shall serve her for that part of her life when that occupation shall have deserted her, a state of things will arrive where a mature woman can abundantly exercise the perfected powers of glorious womanhood; a state of things in which property in the marriage relation will be no more entangled than in any ordinary business partnership between two persons; a state which will lead in time to the desuetude of the dower-right.

When this grand old fortress founded in the feudal ages by mankind and strengthened by them through centuries for the protection of women in the marriage relation, much defaced by the constant attacks of divorce and alimony has become an unused refuge and deserted ruin, grown over with the moss and ivy of tradition, that will be a freer race of women who will contemplate with interest its ancient, massive walls and deep foundations.

Secure in the wider, nobler conditions of independent womanhood she will none the less find her heart most surely at rest in the sacred relationship of marriage with the man of her choice; that one human relationship,

—upon whose tranquil breast
The heads of little children may securely rest.

CPSIA information can be obtained
at www.ICGtesting.com
Printed in the USA
BVHW091313210219
540827BV00022B/1669/P